R
WORD AND PICTURE PUZZLES

Victoria Fremont
and
Ted Lavash

DOVER PUBLICATIONS, INC.
New York

Bibliographical Note

Rebus Word and Picture Puzzles is a new work, first published by Dover Publications, Inc., in 1995.

International Standard Book Number: 0-486-28560-X

Manufactured in the United States of America
Dover Publications, Inc.
31 East 2nd Street
Mineola, N.Y. 11501

How to Read a Rebus

When you see a + (plus) sign, add the letter(s) and the picture together.

t+ 🎩 = that

Or, add the sound of the picture and the letter(s) together.

🔔 +t = belt

When you see a − (minus) sign, subtract the letter(s) from the picture.

🧹 −b = rush   🎩 −h = at

When you see a dark capital letter, pronounce it the way it sounds in the alphabet.

I   C   U = I see you.

An OK Rainy Day

" 👁 hate 🌧+y days," said Isa+🔔 **2** Fran+🗝 , "there isn't **N E** thing **2** do!"

" 🏚 ," said Fran+🗝 , "let's th+ 🍶(INK) . There must 🐝 something we 🥫 do.

R U hungry?" he asked.

"Yes, am. **Y** don't

we make lunch **2**gether?"

asked Isa+ .

"T+'s a great , "

cried Fran+ . "Let's **C**

what's in the kit+."

They +th +ted

2 cook and h+🔑 is w+🎩

they **8 4** lunch.

    Fran+🔑 had a 🎀+L

of 🍲, a **P**nut butter

sand+🧙, a 🍐, some

apple 🥧, and a cup of **T**.

Isa+🔔 had 🍎 juice, **2**na

🐟 salad, 🚗+rots,

a +berry +dae,

and some +k.

After they had **E10**,

they +ed TV. L8er

they told stories and

played .

"**U** know," said Isa+,

" +y days can be OK."

8

Sayings and Superstitions

If you b+🧹 a mirror, you'll have **7** y+🐚+s of bad luck.

An 🍎 a day 🔑+ps the doctor away.

Don't  ...

Don't 👁💧 over spilled 🏭+k.

_____

⚫-b that glitters is 🪢 gold.

_____

A ⌚+ed pot never boils.

_____

Don't count your 🐤🐤

🐝+4 they 🎩+ch.

Birds of a 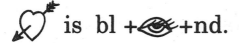 f+🔒 **2**gether.

❤️ is bl +👁+nd.

Sticks and s+🦶+nes may

b+🧹 m+👁 bones, but

names 🥫 never h+🔥

me.

Annabel's New Friends

 U write the names of

-b of the new friends

Anna+🔔 made at her new

school?

1. 🚗 +men _____

2. 🐝 +trice _____

3.  +ton _____

4.  +rene _____

5. ![fan] +y _____

6. ![bone] -br _____

7. Fran+ ![key] _____

8. ![can with brush] +dy _____

9. ![club] +mer _____

10. Gr+ ![ace card] _____

Max's Wish

1 day M+ saw an **L**f.

The **L**f +ld M+ that

he give him 1 wish

would come true.

M+ was **D**+ -+ed.

He closed his +s, **B**gan **2**

th+![ink bottle], and made a wish.

When he o+![pen] +ed his ![eye] +s

he heard a bark. He ![saw] a

![tie] +ny gray puppy n+![ear]

his feet. M+![axe] was so

![hat] -t+py that he ![star] +ted

to ![crying eyes].

    M+![axe] called his puppy

Smo+ 🔑. Every day he

 walk Smo+ 🔑 4

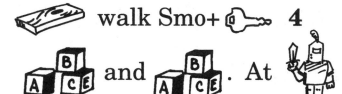 and . At

Smo+ 🔑 would sleep on

M+ 's . M+ had

a friend 4ever!

Jokes and Riddles

1. W+ 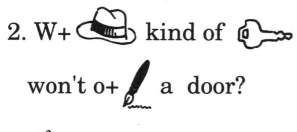 animal is at

every base+ game?

A bat.

2. W+ kind of

won't o+ a door?

A monkey.

3. **Y** didn't the 🐔 cross

the road?

The light was red.

4. What kind of 🎀 can 🪢

B tied?

A rainbow.

5. W+🎩 is green and 🦟+s?

Super pickle.

6. What kind of  does a

t+ have?

An engineer.

7. What did one say **2**

the other?

Nice not to see you again.

8. **Y** is a ba+ like a ?

They both have rattles.

A Letter to Ellen

Dear **LN**,

I'm sorry **2** h+ that

U R sick in with the

+pox. Do **U** have a lot

of spots?

M+ mother says they

will  away in a few

days, and you'll 🐝 back

in school and feeling

🪭 +tastic in no 🕐.

   The teacher says 🪢

2 worry. 👃 +L says **U**

R luc+🔑 because **U**

don't have **N E** homework.

+ny says she has a +t

4 U.

J+ went

+ling **2**day and hurt

his **L**bow, but the

says he 't miss school,

and his pain will s+

soon.

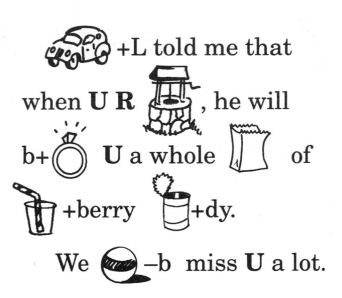

🚗+L told me that when **U R** 🕳️(well), he will b+💍 **U** a whole 🛍️(bag) of 🥤(straw)+berry 🥫(can)+dy.

We 🎱(8 ball)–b miss **U** a lot.

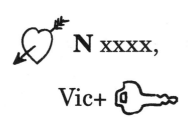

💘 **N** <u>xxxx</u>,

Vic+🔑

Find out what's at the beach by drawing lines from left to right.

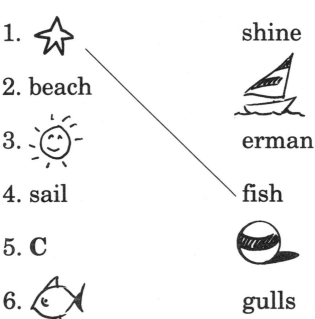

1. ☆   shine

2. beach

3. ☼   erman

4. sail   fish

5. C

6. 🐟   gulls

Find out what's at home
by drawing lines from left to
right.

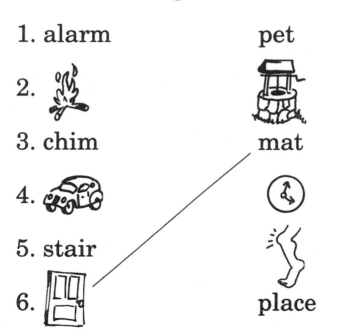

1. alarm   pet

2. [fire]

3. chim   mat

4. [car]   [clock]

5. stair   [foot]

6. [door]   place

Crossword

Across	Down
1. +dy	2. ad+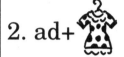
5.	3. ele+ +t
7. st+	4. +works
8. tur+	6. +man
9. note+	

27

At the Zoo

 you find out w+

Rose  at the zoo?

1. ![tie] +ger

2. Mon+![key]

3. Ele+![fan]+t

4. +da

5. +deer

6. Hippo+ +amus

7. -c+ -t+ceros

8. -f+on

9. Ca+

10. H+ +se

11. +guin

Can you find the animals by drawing lines from left to right?

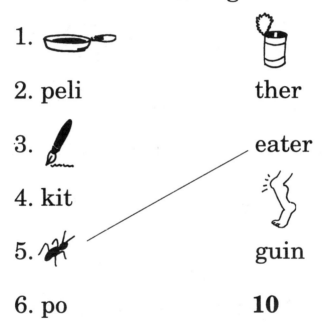

1.

2. peli   ther

3.   eater

4. kit

5.

6. po   guin

10

Can you find the toys by drawing lines from left to right?

1.

2. base   set

3. doll

4. t+   gloves

5. slin   truck

6. 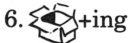+ing

Crossword

Across	Down
2.  +hook	1. +mat
4. +me	3. chim+
7. mit+**10**	5. +da
9. 	6. row+
10. pota+ 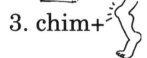	8. tea+

33

What's the Word?

MT _ _ _ _ _

NE _ _ _

LF8r _ _ _ _ _ _ _ _

EZ _ _ _ _

LFNt _ _ _ _ _ _ _ _

B4 _ _ _ _ _ _

E10 _ _ _ _ _

NV _ _ _ _

IV _ _ _

IC _ _ _

RmE _ _ _ _

NrG _ _ _ _ _ _

NME _ _ _ _ _

A Love Letter

On Valentine's day

Lor+ got a -g note

from a **C**cret admirer. This

is w+ he told her:

Roses are -b,

Violets **R** + cy.

If you'll **B** my sweet ,

I'll bring **U** some +dy!

Lor+  wrote

I'll **B** your sweet ♡

just **4** the candy.

I know your +writing,

And your name is Andy!

P.S.  U like **2** come **2**

my on +day?

Find all the 'things that go' by drawing lines from left to right.

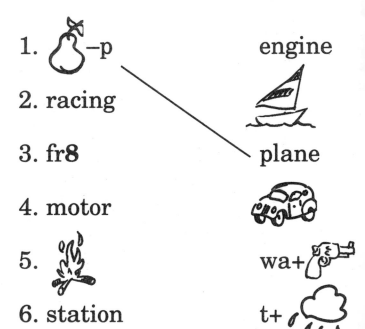

1. –p
2. racing
3. fr**8**
4. motor
5. 
6. station

engine

plane

wa+

t+

Find what's at the hardware store by drawing lines from left to right.

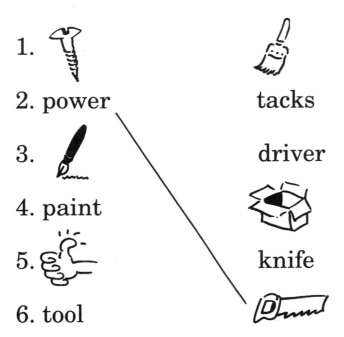

1.

2. power

3.

4. paint

5.

6. tool

tacks

driver

knife

Crossword

Across

1. f+

6. 🖐+kerchief

8. 💤-se

9. 👄

10. toma+🦶

Down

2. 🐔

3. pine+🍎

4. 👞+lace

5. 👍+tack

7. 👁+brow

41

The Tooth Fairy

When 👣+ny lost his 🦷,

his mom said, "👁 th+🍾INK

U should put it under your

🛏️ and a fairy will 🦟

in**2** your 🛏️+room and

b+💍 **U** a gift." 👣+ny didn't

b+[leaf]-s her. He 4got about

the [tooth] and left it on his

[hanger]+er.

    That [robot] [foot]+ny dreamt

that a terrible gi+[ant] [tie]+d

up a lovely fairy and 8 the [tooth].

[foot]+ny jumped out of [bed],

[bee]+gan looking 4 his [tooth],

and put it under his [pillow] .

When [foot]+ny woke up, he

found **2** shiny [25¢]+s in his

[bed] , but he wasn't [table] -t

to find his [tooth]. "Well, maybe

there is a [tooth] fairy," **1**dered

[foot]+ny. "Who [swirl] ?"

Jokes and Riddles

1. W+ did the big

   cracker say to the little one?

   My pop is bigger than your pop.

2. How do you know +rots

   R good 4 your ?

   Ever seen a rabbit with eyeglasses?

3. How do +s their hair?

With a honeycomb.

4. **Y** do cows have +s?

Their horns don't work.

5. What do **U** call +ny dogs in +vania?

Puppies.

46

6. Which do **U** stir your

chocolate +k with?

Neither, I use a spoon.

7. How many monkeys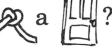

you put in an **MT** ?

One, after that the box isn't empty.

8. When is a door a ?

When it's ajar.

Crossword

Across	Down
3. +barrow	1. tu+👄-s
5. s+🪀	2. 🔔+t
6. 🖊+cil	4. rain+🎀
8. dra+🔫	5. 🌞+dae
9. 🪙	7. 〰+y

48

A Ride in a Tow Truck

1 morning Mr.and Mrs.

La+ 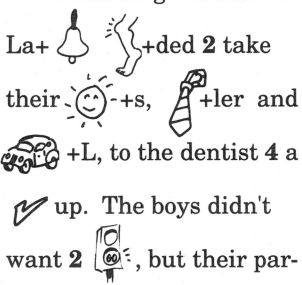 +ded **2** take

their -☺-+s, +ler and

+L, to the dentist **4** a

up. The boys didn't

want **2** , but their parents insisted. They ◯-b

got in2 the 🚗, but after

a few 🧊[ABCE] they heard a

very st+☁+ge 👍+p.

Mr. La+🔔 o+🖊+ed the

🚪 and ⭐+ted 2 look

around. He [saw] that the

right r+[ear] tire was flat.

He looked in the trunk, but

he didn't have a s+🍐.

   "**O,** no," said Mr. La+🔔,

"we won't **B**  -t **2** go **2**

the dentist. I'll have to call

a 🦶 truck." Mr. La+🔔

saw a phone on the corner.

" be h+🐍 in twenty

minutes," he 🍒🍒+d.

When the truck arrived,
Mic+🗝, the driver, asked
if the boys 🪵 like **2**
ride with him. W+🎩a❓!
A ride in a 🦶 truck could
🪢 com+🍐 **2** a visit **2**
the dentist!

Answers

An OK Rainy Day   (pp. 5-8)

"I hate rainy days," said Isabel to Franky, "there isn't anything to do!"

"Well," said Franky, "let's think. There must be something we can do. Are you hungry?" he asked.

"Yes, I am. Why don't we make lunch together?" asked Isabel.

"That's a great idea," cried Franky. "Let's see what's in the kitchen."

They both started to cook and here is what they ate for lunch.

Franky had a bowl of soup, a peanut butter sandwich, a pear, some apple pie, and a cup of tea. Isabel had apple juice, tuna fish salad, carrots, a strawberry sundae, and some milk.

After they had eaten, they watched TV. Later they told ghost stories and played cards.

"You know," said Isabel, "rainy days can be OK."

Sayings and Superstitions (pp. 9-11)

If you break a mirror, you'll have seven years of bad luck.

An apple a day keeps the doctor away.

Don't cry over spilled milk.

All that glitters is not gold.

A watched pot never boils.

Don't count your chickens before they hatch.

Birds of a feather flock together.

Love is blind.

Sticks and stones may break my bones, but names can never harm me.

Annabel's New Friends (pp. 12-13)

Can you write the names of all of the new friends Annabel made at her new school?

1. Carmen 2. Beatrice 3. Milton 4. Irene 5. Fanny 6. Ed 7. Franky 8. Candy 9. Homer 10. Grace

Max's Wish (pp. 14-16)

One day Max saw an elf. The elf told Max that he would give him one wish which would come true.

Max was delighted. He closed his eyes, began to think,

and made a wish. When he opened his eyes he heard a
bark. He saw a tiny gray puppy near his feet. Max was so
happy that he started to cry.

Max called his puppy Smoky. Every day he would walk
Smoky for blocks and blocks. At night Smoky would sleep
on Max's bed. Max had a friend forever!

Jokes and Riddles   (pp. 17-19)

What animal is at every baseball game? A bat.
What kind of key won't open a door? A monkey.
Why didn't the chicken cross the road? The light was red.
What kind of bow cannot be tied? A rainbow.
What is green and flies? Super pickle.
What kind of ear does a train have? An engineer.
What did one ghost say to the other? Nice not to see
you again.
Why is a baby like a car? They both have rattles.

A Letter to Ellen   (pp. 20-23)

Dear Ellen,
I'm sorry to hear that you are sick in bed with the chicken
pox. Do you have a lot of spots?

My mother says they will go away in a few days, and you'll be back in school and feeling fantastic in no time.

The teacher says not to worry. Paul says you are lucky because you don't have any homework.

Penny says she has a treat for you.

Jason went bowling today and hurt his elbow, but the nurse says he can't miss school, and his pain will stop soon.

Carl told me that when you are well, he will bring you a whole bag of strawberry candy.

We all miss you a lot.

Love and kisses,
Vicki

Find out what's at the beach by drawing lines from left to right. (p. 24)

l. starfish 2. beach ball 3. sunshine 4. sailboat 5. seagulls 6. fisherman

Find out what's at home by drawing lines
from left to right.   (p. 25)
1. alarm clock 2. fireplace 3. chimney 4. carpet 5.
stairwell 6. doormat

Crossword   (pp. 26-27)
Across: 1. candy 5. typewriter 7. string 8. turkey
          9. notebook
Down: 2. address 3. elephant 4. fireworks 6. Batman

At the Zoo   (pp. 28-29)
Can you find out what Rose saw at the zoo?
1. tiger 2. monkey 3. elephant 4. panda 5. reindeer
6. hippopotamus 7. rhinoceros 8. lion 9. camel 10. horse
11. penguin

Can you find the animals by drawing lines
from left to right?   (p. 30)
1. panther 2. pelican 3. penguin 4. kitten 5. anteater
6. pony

Can you find the toys by drawing lines from left to right?   (p. 31)
1. fire truck 2. baseball 3. doll house 4. train set 5. slinky
6. boxing gloves

Crossword   (pp. 32-33)
Across: 2. fishhook 4. home 7. mitten 9. bed 10. potato
Down: 1. doormat 3. chimney 5. panda 6. rowboat
             8. teacup

What's the Word?   (pp. 34-35)
empty, any, elevator, easy, elephant, before, eaten, envy,
ivy, icy, army, energy, enemy

A Love Letter   (pp. 36-37)
On Valentine's Day Lorraine got a love note from a secret
admirer. This is what he told her:

Roses are red, violets are fancy. If you'll be my sweetheart, I'll bring you some candy!

Lorraine wrote back:

I'll be your sweetheart, not just for the candy. I know your handwriting, and your name is Andy!

P.S. Would you like to come to my house on Sunday?

Find all the 'things that go' by drawing lines from left to right. (p. 38)
1. airplane 2. racing car 3. freight train 4. motorboat
5. fire engine 6. station wagon

Find what's at the hardware store by drawing lines from left to right. (p. 39)
1. screwdriver 2. power saw 3. pen knife 4. paint brush
5. thumbtacks 6. tool box

Crossword (pp. 40-41)
Across: 1. face 6. handkerchief 8. no 9. lips 10. tomato
Down: 2. chicken 3. pineapple 4. shoelace 5. thumb-
tack 7. eyebrow

The Tooth Fairy (pp. 42-44)
When Tony lost his tooth, his mom said, "I think you should put it under your pillow and a fairy will fly into your bedroom and bring you a gift." Tony didn't believe

her. He forgot about the tooth and left it on his dresser.

That night Tony dreamt that a terrible giant tied up a lovely fairy and ate the tooth. Tony jumped out of bed, began looking for his tooth, and put it under his pillow.

When Tony woke up, he found two shiny quarters in his bed, but he wasn't able to find his tooth. "Well, maybe there is a tooth fairy," wondered Tony. "Who knows?"

Jokes and Riddles (pp. 45-47)

1. What did the big firecracker say to the little one? My pop is bigger than your pop.
2. How do you know carrots are good for your eyes? Ever seen a rabbit with eyeglasses?
3. How do bees comb their hair? With a honeycomb.
4. Why do cows have bells? Their horns don't work.
5. What do you call tiny dogs in Pennsylvania? Puppies.
6. Which hand do you stir your chocolate milk with? Neither, I use a spoon.
7. How many monkeys can you put in an empty box? One, after that the box isn't empty.
8. When is a door not a door? When it's ajar.

Crossword (pp. 48-49)

Across: 3. wheelbarrow 5. stop 6. pencil 8. dragon
9. penny

Down: 1. tulip 2. belt 4. rainbow 5. sundae 7. army

A Ride in a Tow Truck (pp. 50-53)

One morning Mr. and Mrs. Labell needed to take their sons, Tyler and Carl, to the dentist for a checkup. The boys didn't want to go, but their parents insisted. They all got into the car, but after a few blocks they heard a very strange thump. Mr. Labell opened the door and started to look around. He saw that the right rear tire was flat. He looked in the trunk, but he didn't have a spare.

"Oh, no," said Mr. Labell, "we won't be able to go to the dentist. I'll have to call a tow truck." Mr. Labell saw a phone on the corner. "He'll be here in twenty minutes," he cried.

When the truck arrived, Mickey, the driver, asked if the boys would like to ride with him. What a question! A ride in a tow truck could not compare to a visit to the dentist!